South Carolina

ABC Coloring Book

An ABC Learning Activity Book all about South Carolina

With Count-to-10 Coloring Bonus!

Little Red Hills

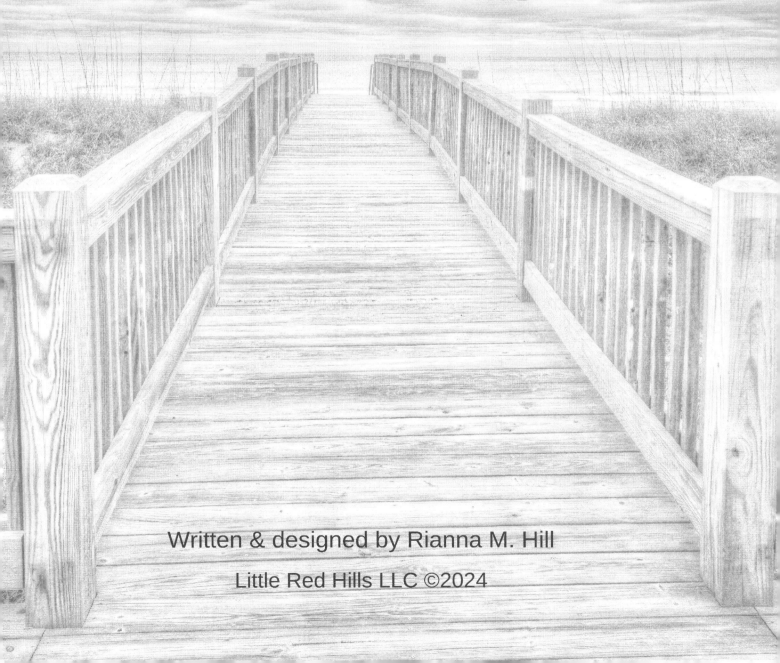

Written & designed by Rianna M. Hill

Little Red Hills LLC ©2024

My ABCs
South Carolina
Coloring Book

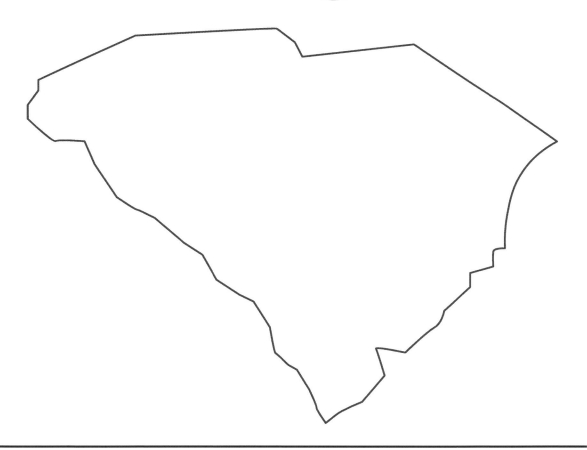

name: _____

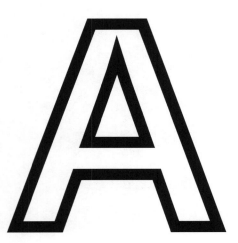

Alligator

Commonly found in swamps and
wetlands, alligators are large reptiles.
They inhabit various freshwater
habitats in South Carolina.

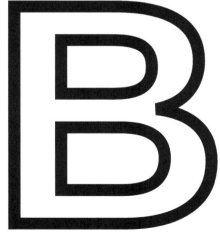

B

Beach

South Carolina is famous for its beautiful, white sand beaches including Hunting Island State Park Beach, Folly Island, Fripp Island Beach, Myrtle Beach State Park, and Fish Haul Beach Park.

C

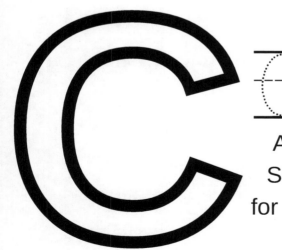

Charleston

A beautiful, historic town on the coast of South Carolina, Charleston is well known for its historic houses, beautiful bridges, and beaches.

D

Darlington
Raceway

Known as "The Track Too Tough to Tame,"
this famous NASCAR track in Darlington,
South Carolina is one of the oldest and most
iconic race tracks in the country.

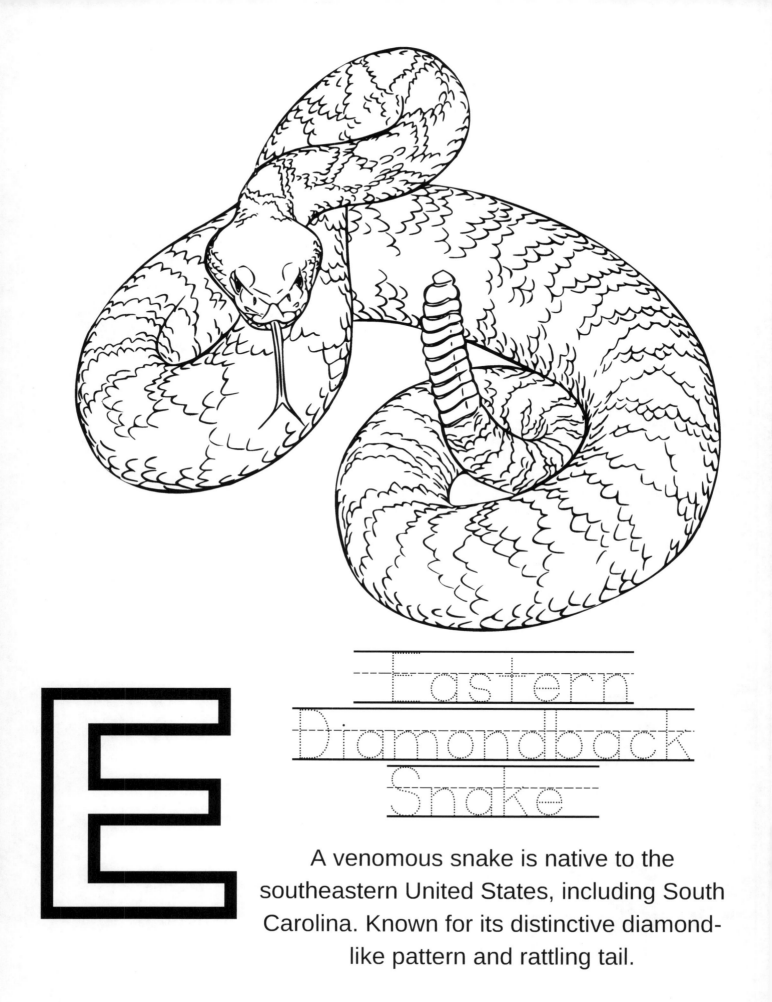

E

Eastern
Diamondback
Snake

A venomous snake is native to the
southeastern United States, including South
Carolina. Known for its distinctive diamond-
like pattern and rattling tail.

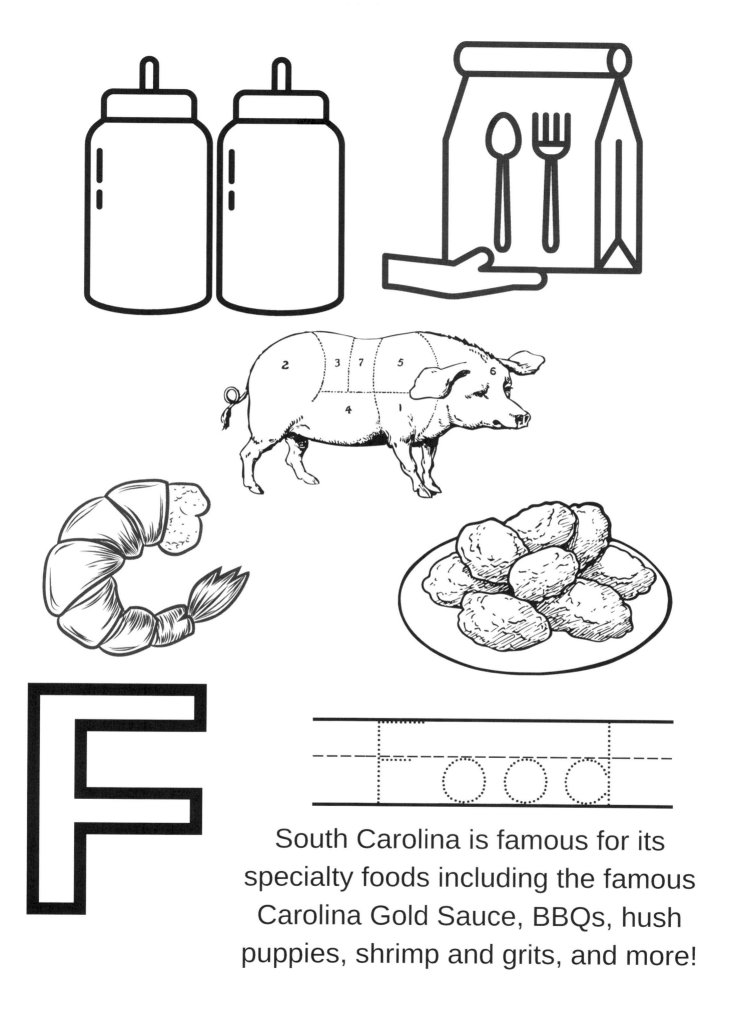

South Carolina is famous for its specialty foods including the famous Carolina Gold Sauce, BBQs, hush puppies, shrimp and grits, and more!

G

Golf

South Carolina is well known for its many beautiful and famous gold courses. It is often called the "Birthplace of American Golf"

H

Hawk

Various species of hawks inhabit South Carolina, including the red-tailed hawk and Cooper's hawk. They are birds of prey known for their sharp vision and hunting skills.

I

Indigo Snake

The Eastern Indigo snake, the longest native snake in North America, can be found in South Carolina. It's non-venomous and plays a crucial role in the ecosystem.

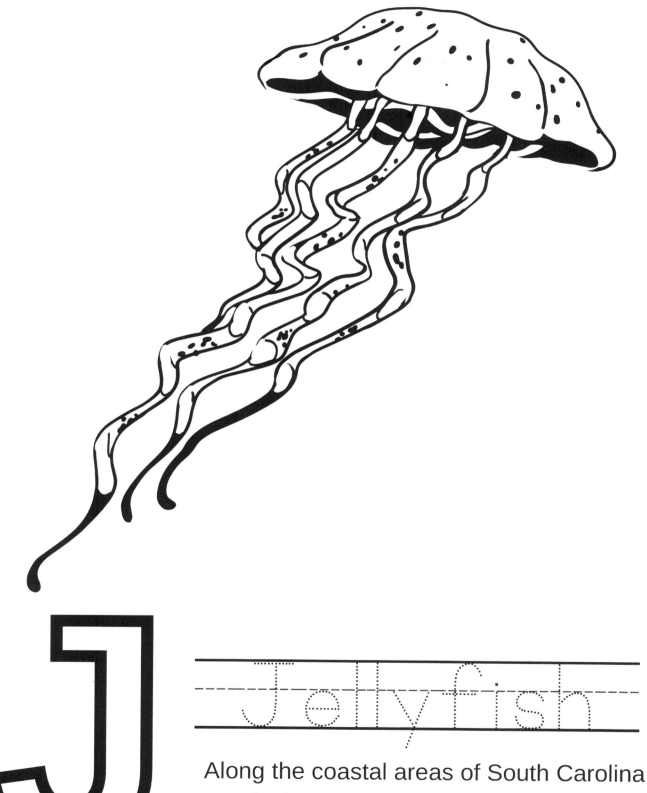

J

Jellyfish

Along the coastal areas of South Carolina, particularly in the Atlantic Ocean, various species of jellyfish can be found, including the moon jellyfish and cannonball jellyfish.

K

Kestrel

The American kestrel, a small and colorful falcon, can be spotted in South Carolina. They hover while hunting for small mammals and insects.

L

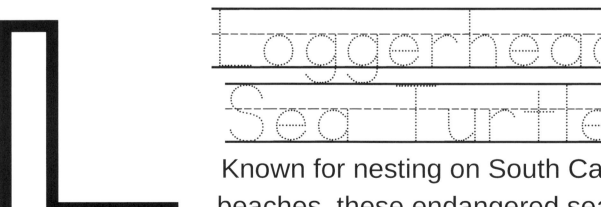

Known for nesting on South Carolina's beaches, these endangered sea turtles are large and have reddish-brown shells.

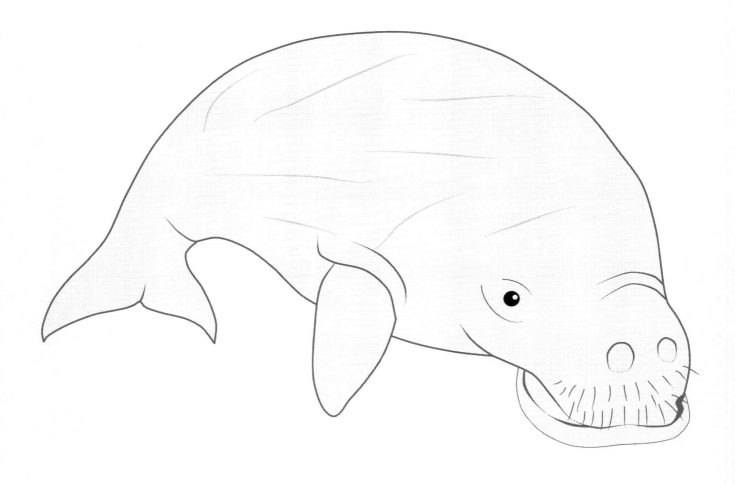

M

Manatee

Occasional visitors to South Carolina's coastal waters, manatees are large aquatic mammals often seen grazing on seagrasses.

This large rodent is semi-aquatic
living in wetlands and eat primatily
aquatic plants and roots.

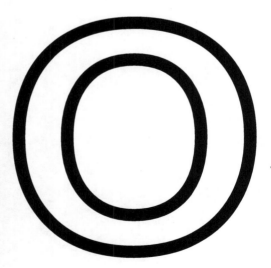

Opossum

These marsupials are common throughout South Carolina. They have distinctive rat-like tails and are known for "playing dead" when threatened.

P Palmetto

South Carolina is known as the
Palmetto State. The official state tree
is the Sabal palmetto.

Q

Quail

Both Bobwhite quail and other species are found in South Carolina, often inhabiting grasslands, fields, and brushy areas.

R

Raccoon

Easily recognizable with their bandit-like facial markings, raccoons are adaptable and can be found in various habitats across the state.

S

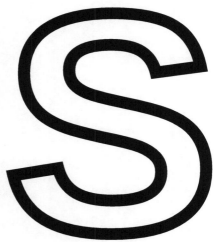

Snapping
Turtle

These freshwater turtles have powerful jaws and can be found in ponds, lakes, and slow-moving streams in South Carolina.

T

Tiger Swallowtail Butterfly

This large and striking butterfly with yellow and black stripes can be seen fluttering through gardens and woodlands in South Carolina.

Upland
Sandpiper

During migration, these slender shorebirds with long necks and legs can be spotted in grasslands and agricultural fields of South Carolina.

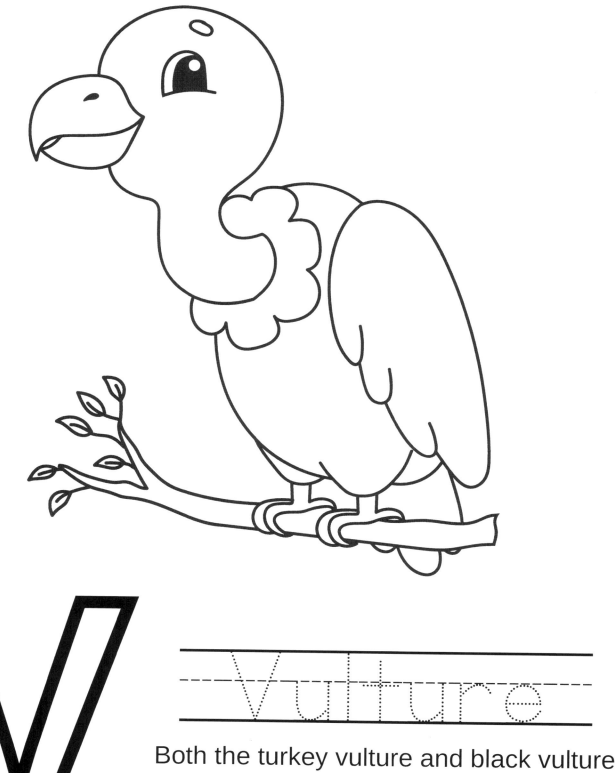

V

Vulture

Both the turkey vulture and black vulture are found in South Carolina. They are scavengers and play an important role in cleaning up carrion.

Wood Duck

Colorful and highly ornamented wood ducks are commonly found in wetlands and wooded swamps throughout South Carolina.

X

Xandra Court

Xandra Court is a residential street in Fort Mill, South Carolina with high preforming schools and a rich history.

Y

Yellow Branch Falls

This stunning natural attraction offers a moderately challenging hike leading to a 50-foot cascade surrounded by lush greenery.

Z

Zydeco Events

Zydeco music and dance events
occasionally take place in the state.
These events celebrate the lively Creole
music and dance style.

MY COUNT TO 10 SOUTH CAROLINA COLORING BOOK

name:

1

one raccoon

2

two turtles

three alligators

5

five sandpipers

six butterflies

7

seven quails

8

eight birds

9

nine vultures

10

ten sand

dollars

Thank you for supporting our small family business!

Learn more at:

www.LittleRedHills.com

Questions or
suggestions for improvement?
Rianna@LittleRedHills.com

Wholesale order questions for
your shop?
Rianna@LittleRedHills.com

Made in United States
Orlando, FL
21 July 2025